Kipsigis

D1544591

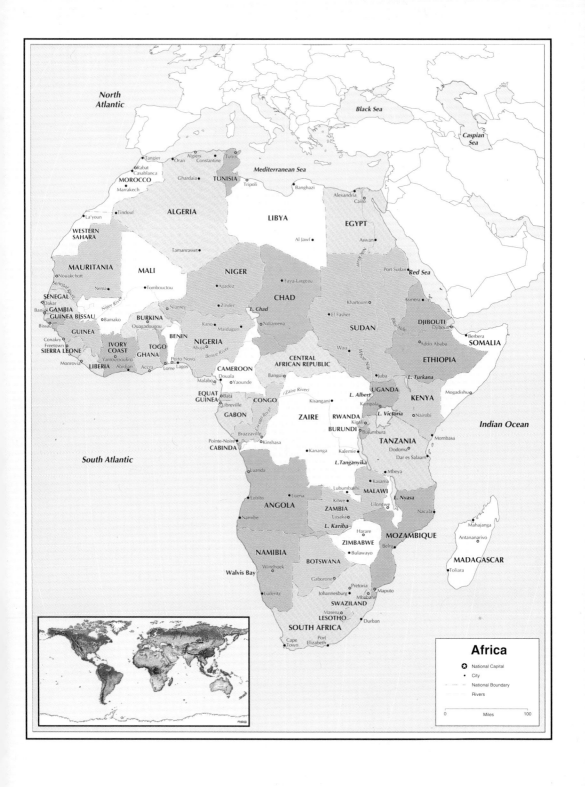

North
Atlantic

Black Sea

Caspian
Sea

Tangier
Algiers Constantine Tunisi
Oran
Rabat
Casablanca
Ghardaia
Marrakech

MOROCCO

Mediterranean Sea

TUNISIA
Tripoli
Banghazi
Alexandria
Cairo

La'youn
Tindouf

ALGERIA

LIBYA

EGYPT

**WESTERN
SAHARA**

Tamanrasset
Al Jawf
Aswan

MAURITANIA
Nouakchott
Nema
MALI
Tombouctou

NIGER
Agadez
Faya-Largeau
Port Sudan
Red Sea

Berbera

SENEGAL
Dakar
Senegal River
Niger River
Niamey
Zinder
CHAD
Khartoum
Asmera

GAMBIA
Banjul
GUINEA BISSAU
Bissau
Bamako
Kano
Maidugun
Ndjamena
El Fasher
El Obeid
DJIBOUTI
Djibouti

GUINEA
Conakry
Freetown
SIERRA LEONE
Ouagadougou
BURKINA
BENIN
NIGERIA
Ahuja
Benue River
Wau
SUDAN
Addis Ababa
SOMALIA

**IVORY
COAST**
Yamoussoukro
TOGO
GHANA
Porto Novo
Lome Lagos
**CENTRAL
AFRICAN REPUBLIC**
White Nile
Blue Nile
ETHIOPIA

Monrovia
LIBERIA
Abidjan
Accra
CAMEROON
Douala
Yaounde
Bangui
Juba
L. Turkana
Mogadishu

**EQUAT
GUINEA**
Malabo
Bata
CONGO
(Zaire River)
Kisangani
L. Albert
UGANDA
KENYA
Kampala

GABON
Libreville
ZAIRE
RWANDA
Kigali
L. Victoria
Nairobi

Brazzaville
Congo River
BURUNDI
Bujumbura
Indian Ocean

Pointe-Noire
Kinshasa
Kananga
Kalemie
TANZANIA
Dodoma
Mombasa

South Atlantic
CABINDA
Dar es Salaam

Luanda
L.Tanganyika
Mbeya

Lubumbashi
Kasama

Luena
Kitwe
MALAWI
L. Nyasa
Nacala

Lobito
ZAMBIA
Lilongwe

ANGOLA
Lusaka
L. Kariba
Mahajanga

Nambe
Harare
MOZAMBIQUE
Antananarivo

ZIMBABWE
Beira

NAMIBIA
Bulawayo
MADAGASCAR

Windhoek
BOTSWANA
Toliara

Walvis Bay

Luderitz
Gaborone
Pretoria
Maputo
Johannesburg
Mbabane
SWAZILAND
Maseru
LESOTHO
Durban

SOUTH AFRICA
Cape
Town
Port
Elizabeth

Africa

⊕ National Capital
• City
- - - National Boundary
— Rivers

0   Miles   100

The Heritage Library of African Peoples

KIPSIGIS

Abdul Karim Bangura, Ph.D.

THE ROSEN PUBLISHING GROUP, INC.
NEW YORK

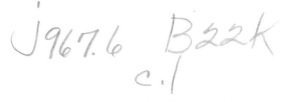

J967.6 B22k
c.1

Published in 1994 by The Rosen Publishing Group, Inc.
29 East 21st Street, New York, NY 10010

Copyright 1994 by The Rosen Publishing Group, Inc.

All rights reserved. No part of this book may be reproduced in any form without permission in writing from the publisher, except by a reviewer.

First Edition

Manufactured in the United States of America

Library of Congress Cataloging-in-Publication Data

Bangura, Abdul Karim, 1953–
   Kipsigis / Abdul Karim Bangura. — 1st ed.
     p. cm. — (The Heritage library of African peoples)
   Includes bibliographical references and index.
   ISBN 0-8239-1765-7
   1. Kipsigis (African people)—Juvenile literature. [1. Kipsigis (African people)] I. Title. II. Series.
DT433.545.K57B36   1994
960'.04965—dc20   94-16188
                                        CIP
                                        AC

Contents

Introduction   6

1.   The People of This Place   9

2.   Kipsigisland   14

3.   The Organization of Society   19

4.   Initiation   28

5.   Marriage and Family   36

6.   European Contact and
     Colonial Rule   46

7.   A View of the Future   54

     Glossary   59

     For Further Reading   60

     Index   62

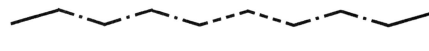

INTRODUCTION

THERE IS EVERY REASON FOR US TO KNOW something about Africa and to understand its past and the way of life of its peoples. Africa is a rich continent that has for centuries provided the world with art, culture, labor, wealth, and natural resources. It has vast mineral deposits, fossil fuels, and commercial crops.

But perhaps most important is the fact that fossil evidence indicates that human beings originated in Africa. The earliest traces of human beings and their tools are almost two million years old. Their descendants have migrated throughout the world. To be human is to be of African descent.

The experiences of the peoples who stayed in Africa are as rich and as diverse as of those who established themselves elsewhere. This series of books describes their environment, their modes of subsistence, their relationships, and their customs and beliefs. The books present the variety of languages, histories, cultures, and religions that are to be found on the African continent. They demonstrate the historical linkages between African peoples and the way contemporary Africa has been affected by European colonial rule.

Africa is large, complex, and diverse. It encompasses an area of more than 11,700,000 square miles. The United States, Europe, and India could fit easily into it. The sheer size is an indication of the continent's great variety in geography, terrain, climate, flora, fauna, peoples, languages, and cultures.

Much of contemporary Africa has been shaped by European colonial rule, industrialization, urbanization, and the demands of a world economic system. For more than seventy years, large regions of Africa were ruled by Great Britain, France, Belgium, Portugal, and Spain. African peoples from various ethnic, linguistic, and cultural backgrounds were brought together to form colonial states.

For decades Africans struggled to gain their independence. It was not until after World War II that the colonial territories became independent African states. Today, almost all of Africa is ruled by Africans. Large numbers of Africans live in modern cities. Rural Africa is also being transformed, and yet its people still engage in many of their age-old customs, practices, and beliefs.

Contemporary circumstances and natural events have not always been kind to ordinary Africans. Today, however, new social movements and technological innovations pose great promise for future development.▲

George C. Bond
Institute of African Studies
Columbia University, New York

The Kipsigis are one of the many peoples of eastern Africa.

chapter

1

THE PEOPLE OF THIS PLACE

LONG AGO A PEOPLE TRAVELED FROM THE north. They traveled for a long time, but finally one day they met an old woman sitting on a hill. She was weaving a basket, which she called a kisgisik. *The people settled in this land and were called* Kipsigis, *after the baskets that they still weave today.*

This is one of many stories used to explain the origin of the name Kipsigis. The people called Kipsigis live in the western part of Kenya.

The Nile River flows from Sudan through Egypt into the Mediterranean Sea. The Kipsigis migrated from the region of the Upper Nile valley in present-day Egypt, through Sudan, down to Mount Elgon and Lake Baringo, and finally settling in the Kericho District.

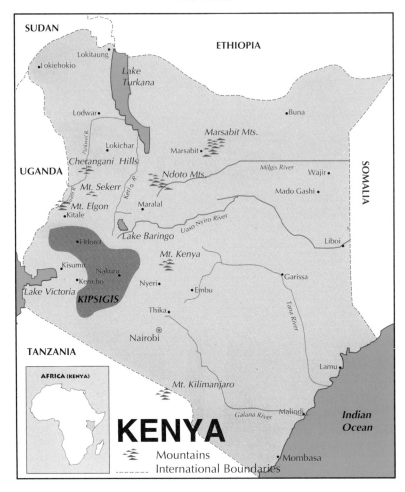

The area was inhabited when the Kipsigis arrived. They learned the traditions of the original peoples and traded with them. However, when they tried to drive out the people known as Gusii, serious fighting took place. In the middle of the 18th century, the Kipsigis defeated the Gusii at the battle of Chemoiben.

Some Kipsigis remained in the region; others continued to move southward into the Sot region. There, they encountered the Maasai.

KIPSIGIS MIGRATION ROUTE

——— Rivers
Kenya
Kipsigis
·········· Kipsigis Migration Route

After many battles, the Maasai drove the Kipsigis beyond the Amala River into present-day Kipsigis territory.

Kipsigis have steadily grown in numbers. In 1939, the population was 80,000. By 1981, the Kipsigis population had reached 500,000.

▼ LANGUAGE ▼

The Kipsigis language is a form of Nandi. It belongs to the Kalenjin language group, which includes the languages spoken by the Nandi, Terik, Keiyu, Tugen, Marakwet, Pokot, Sabaot, and other groups.

11

The Kipsigis population has steadily grown. They number over 500,000 today.

The Kipsigis and Nandi languages are understood by both ethnic groups, but each group worried that its language might be lost or changed, fearing cultural domination.

As a result, a Kipsigis-Nandi Language Committee was formed to give each language equal prominence. This solution worked quite well. Both groups accepted "Kalenjin" as a name for both languages.

KALENJIN ORAL TRADITIONS

The Kalenjin language was never written down until 1903. How did people remember stories and songs and news before they could be written down? They had an "oral tradition." Songs, verses, prayers, stories, curses, and even history were taught to children by their parents and grandparents. The children remembered these things all their lives and taught them to their own kids. Here are some examples of Kalenjin oral traditions.

Proverbs

Menemugei chi met. (One cannot shave one's own hair.) We all must help each other out.

Murchechang mobole kering. (Too many rats can't dig a hole.) Group projects must be organized or nothing will get done.

Riddles

Who am I?

Q: *Nyelnyel kou chepseyan.* As flexible as a wristband.

A: *Even.* A snake.

Q: *Pilipili me tabot.* Pepper on the ceiling.

A: *Solob.* Cockroaches.

Curses

Wechin peik. May water make you ill.

Wechin mat. May fire harm you.

Ikubwi. May you fall on your head.▲

chapter

2

KIPSIGISLAND

KIPSIGISLAND IS THE HIGHLAND REGION IN THE Kericho District of western Kenya. The original Kipsigis reserve covered an area of 821 square miles. In 1930, an area of 148 square miles called Chepalungu was added. The land altitude ranges from 5,000 to 8,000 feet.

The climate is cool, with temperatures ranging from 36F to 95F. Rainfall is plentiful, with an average of 139 rainy days a year. In fact, when young men learn the art of "rainmaking," it is more important for them to learn to stop the rain rather than to start it. The land and the climatic conditions are excellent for growing tea, pyrethrum (a plant used as insect spray by farmers) and corn, and for raising cattle.

Kipsigisland is rich in ash from extinct volcanoes. When the ash was observed to attract cattle, the Kipsigis decided that it must be im-

The Kipsigis paint sacred markings on their faces and bodies with substances such as ash and a fine white clay called kaolin.

portant for humans, too. Ash is used as hair dressing, toothpowder, and the dry paint for sacred markings on face and body. Cow urine is used to wash wooden containers, curdle milk, and warm cold hands on chilly mornings. Ritual objects, jewelry, and kitchen utensils are made of cow bone.

THE MYTH OF THE ORIGIN OF CATTLE

Many years ago the Kipsigis did not have cattle. They didn't even know what a cow was! There was a man who lived near a lake, and every evening he saw creatures coming out of the water and grazing on the banks. When daylight covered the land, the creatures and their young would go back into the water. If the man went near them they did not run away, but kept on grazing. One day the man said, "How shall I catch them and keep them from returning to the lake?" He fenced in a corral, and gave it two gates, one facing the lake, the other facing his house. He let the grass grow over the fence until it could not be seen. Then one night he opened the gate that faced the lake and closed the one that faced his house. That night the cattle came out of the water and grazed so far up the bank that they entered the corral. The man shut the gate that faced the lake, and waited. When the world became day he opened the other gate and drove the cattle home. The people at home thought the cattle were a very good thing because they gave milk. So everyone fenced in corrals. And those who couldn't fence their own prayed for the fortunate ones to share with them, because it was the beginning of the world and everyone was generous. The cattle multiplied, and they are plentiful in Kipsigisland even now.

Life in Kipsigisland before 1889 was largely centered around cattle. Because cattle and related objects have strong ritual value, the herds still remain a major source of wealth. A Kipsigis boy is given his own animal early in life. From this animal's name or its special markings, the boy takes his own name-of-honor, his "ox-name." The ox becomes close to his heart:

He cherishes it, guards it, and carefully grooms it each day. He hangs an iron bell around its neck, twists and hammers its horns into beautiful designs, and composes songs and poems in its honor. When the ox dies, a part of him also dies. If the boy dies young, the ox is sacrificed.

Kipsigis obtain their food from their herds. Milk and blood are prized. Meat is eaten only when an animal dies or is sacrificed in a religious rite. Meat and milk may not be eaten together. From the herds' skins come clothing, bedding, containers, and shelters. Cow dung is used to plaster homes and to make fires.

▼ LAND AND TRADITION ▼

Kipsigisland was traditionally divided into four *emotinwek* (districts), because the number four is sacred to the Kipsigis. These *emotinwek* are known as *Peelkut* (which means "warm mouth," as it is a good area for grazing), *Waldai* (translated as "change right hand"), *Pureti* (named for the Tulu ab Pureti mountain), and *Sot* (named for a Kipsigis hero, Kipsot).

In the traditional cattle-herding economy, all land was owned by everyone. Now the land is divided into two major sections: agricultural land, covering 939,000 acres, and townships, covering 269,000 acres.

The change began in 1889 when the Kipsigis first encountered British colonizers. When the

These children are harvesting pyrethrum, a kind of chrysanthemum that yields an insecticide that is not harmful to humans.

British began seizing the land to give to white settlers, they claimed that their intention was to create a buffer zone between the Kipsigis and the Gusii. But from the start, it was clear to the British that they could make more profit by converting the land from herding to farming.

When Kenya fought for and finally won its independence from Great Britain in 1963, the process of determining land ownership began in Kipsigis country. Since then many disputes have taken place. Because the Kipsigis once believed that the land belonged to everyone, they had no laws dealing with land ownership.▲

chapter

3

THE ORGANIZATION OF SOCIETY

THE EARLY KIPSIGIS WAY OF LIFE NEEDED almost no government. No chief or ruler existed. Kipsigis did not submit to authority of any kind. Tall, proud, always ready to defend their honor, they were (and still are) among the world's staunchest believers in equality. A man could own a thousand cows but still not be considered better than a fellow Kipsigis who had fewer. Yet there was always order in the Kipsigis world. Disputes were settled through mediation within the *kokwet*, or village. Differences between Kipsigis and other ethnic groups could be settled only by war. But even war had rules of behavior: Women and babies must be spared.

Besides their ties of kinship, the Kipsigis had a broader bond that shaped everyday life: the age-set, or *ipinda*, and shared experience. Boys or girls initiated together were expected to be friends for life. Age-mates also trained and fought together in the army.

Kipsigis organize themselves and divide their responsibilities in age-grades, rather than kinship lineage. Kipsigis believe in human equality, especially with respect to social, economic, and political rights and privileges.

▼ THE *IPINDA* (AGE–SET) ▼

Kipsigis define the duties and privileges of each generation by an age-set or *ipinda*. Each age-set goes through a cycle that lasts about 105 years. A new age-set with the same name cannot be opened until it has been shown that all persons who belonged to the previous set have died.

As soon boys come out of initiation at fourteen to eighteen (until recently, the ages ranged from twenty to thirty), they go through a period of seclusion in the bush for nine months. This allows them to be initiated into an age-set.

There are three age-grades: boyhood, warriorhood, and elderhood. When initiated into an age-set, the boys enter at the same time into the age-grade of warriorhood. During his period as a warrior, a youth can bear arms, raid, hunt, attend dances and festivals, and marry.

▼ THE CLAN ▼

The Kipsigis clan is descended through males. Today many clans are scattered through-

While they are confined, boys and girls awaiting initiation must wear a simple, untreated skin and cover their faces with a *nariet*, an eyeshade made with shells and pearls.

out Kipsigisland, although their origins can be traced to a common ancestor. Members of a clan share a sacred animal or totem. Even when they fight among themselves, members of a clan try hard to seem unified to other clans. Clan marks are proudly displayed on the ears of cattle.

▼ WAR AND THE *PURIET* ▼

During the precolonial period, the *Puriet* or army played a prominent part in the lives of the Kipsigis. Battles were won through a combination of sheer numbers and fierce fighting spirit.

The Kipsigis military organization was initially made up of four units or *poriosiek* (since the number four is sacred). The units were assigned according to age-sets, and each unit was associated with a specific region. The four units fought individually, which led to weak and often conflicting strategies.

Later the four units were combined into two armies. One army specialized in fighting, and the other in removing spoils (usually cattle) from the battleground. This also was far from satisfactory; often those who collected the cattle did not want to share the spoils.

The weakness of the two-army system was made clear in a major defeat of the Kipsigis by the Gusii in the mid-nineteenth century. After that defeat, the Kipsigis armies were joined into a single unit. But the army still did not perform well against strong opposition. A combined force of Gusii, Watende, Luo, and Kuria ethnic groups defeated them at Mogori in 1890.

▼ CIVIL AUTHORITY AND LAW ▼

The *kokwet* or village, which serves as the economic unit, is also the basic unit of administration. It plays a significant role in the regulation of economic cooperation and the resolution of disputes. Authority over the village is held by elders. Most disputes arise between members of the same village; therefore the *kokwet* is important in their resolution.

During the colonial period some aspects of the British legal system were introduced in Kenya. Today most cases are handled by the magistrate's court and the police. The *kokwet* is not often used as a court, but it still handles cases of juveniles and first-time offenders.

▼ RELIGION ▼

For the Kipsigis, every aspect of life is a response to the environment. These responses are expressed in the beliefs and rituals that make up their religion. The Kipsigis originally believed in a supreme being or God. They called him *Asis*, which means "sun," but he was not thought to *be* the sun. Rather, like the sun, he was the great creator, sustainer of life, and giver of light, rain, and fertility. Asis had another name, *Ngolo*,

A *kokwotinwek*, or higher judge, wears a special mantle when he meets with the *kokwet*. The spear is his sign of authority. This *kokwotinwek* is pictured with his four most recent wives.

which means "up above." Sometimes, however, Asis and Ngolo were combined and called *Cheptalel*, or "pure white girl." Probably the female god is an older tradition than the male sky god.

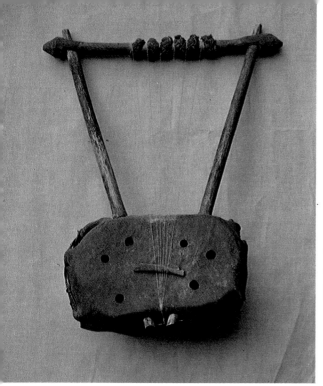

These stringed instruments are made of wood and skin. They are plucked to accompany the beat of a song.

To the Kipsigis, a human being is a spirit in a temporary body. They believe that the spirit is immortal, and that when a body dies its spirit finds new life in a newborn child. Each Kipsigis child is given its own name plus the name of the man or woman who once held the child's spirit.

A high priest, the *Boyot ab Tumda*, officiates at circumcisions, weddings, and other ceremonies. A public worship called *Kapkoros* is held once a year. The priest blesses the congregation by sprinkling them with a mixture of milk and iron oxide. He then recites a prayer that describes all the things most important in Kipsigis life: "Oh, God, give me children and give me cattle and give me millet."

Contemporary Kipsigis society is home to a wide range of beliefs, including the worship of one God, sun worship, totemism (worship of sacred objects), and belief in good and bad spirits.

Magic is still widespread, and some of those who practice it are either feared or respected. A *laibon* is believed to have the power to separate his shadow from his body and to foretell the future. The power of the *ponindet* (traditional magician) is only for evil. The *chebsogeyot* is a female doctor who uses traditional methods to cure people.

KIPSIGIS MUSIC

The Kipsigis learn to sing as children. Songs are taught for ceremonies, for herding cattle, and for harvesting crops. Groups of children, sometimes of fifty or more, learn call-and-answer songs that they sing as games while they work.

A number of musical instruments are used by the Kipsigis. They play a flute called *nduryret* and stringed instruments called *kipugandet* and *ketuba*.

Some Kipsigis songs explain the origins of things. In "Iman and Tengek" ("Truth and Lies"), we learn why one is good and the other bad:

Kingetyo piik oeng, Iman ak
   Tengek.
Kelenjikee ingeruten kebe
   emet
ne loo got,
kole tuwan ingebe.
Konget Iman ak lagokyik lo,
Tengek ak lagokyik somok,
koba ngomii oret kwenet
   komache koimen.
kotebee Iman Tengek
   kolenji
"Kirue ano yeiman?"

Kowalji Tengek kolenji
"arue ketit parak ak
   lagokyuk."
Koba yeimen kolany ketit
   parak
Tengek ak lagokyik
koru ngwong Iman ak
   lagokyik.
Koruiyo ngomi kemoi kwen
kowus isone kotururgee
Tenek ak lagokyik komeiyo
   tugul,
konget ine Iman.
"Ara!" kigila,
"Iman ko kararan
Tengek ko ya."

There were two men, Truth
   and Lies.
They said they would go to
   a faraway country.
They both said, Let's go!

Truth and his six children,
Lies and his three children,
Off they went as night was
   coming on.
Truth asked Lies

"Where will we sleep to-
   night?"

Lies answered, "My chil-
   dren and I
shall sleep under the tree."
When night came, Lies and
his children climbed the
   tree,
Truth and his children lay
   under it.
As they slept at night
the wind blew, and out of
   the tree fell Lies and his
   children, and they died,
but Truth remained.
"Truth must be good,
and Lies are bad." ▲

4

INITIATION

WHEN KIPSIGIS BOYS AND GIRLS HAVE PASSED through puberty, they go through a six-month ritual called initiation. This series of sacred practices prepares them to become responsible adults. Only those who have passed through initiation are called Kipsigis. The uninitiated can only be "children of Kipsigis."

The five elements of the ritual are: (1) circumcision, without which no marriage or sexual relations can be established with other members of the community; (2) initiation into the secret rituals of the community, which helps to create a strong link uniting all Kipsigis; (3) a rite of passage from childhood to adulthood; (4) instruction in tribal customs by the elders; and (5) infliction of bodily pain to harden the physical endurance of youngsters.

Circumcision is a trial of physical endurance

Boys create their own attire for the circumcision ritual.

and bravery. According to myth, a stranger in Kipsigisland once behaved in an offensive way. To punish him, the elders took him to a hill and circumcised him, leaving him there to die. But instead of dying, the man lived a healthy life. He married, had many children, and won many cattle. Because he was so prosperous, the Kipsigis decided that everyone should be circumcised. That hill is now called Tuluap Lagoi (hill of the children).

About a month after circumcision comes the second ceremony, the rite of cleansing, known as the "dipping of the hands." The initiates have been forbidden to touch or eat food or other things for an entire month. Now they dip their hands into a basin containing tools and sacred objects, after which they can touch many of the things that were once forbidden to them.

The third ceremony of initiation is the teaching of rules of behavior. The lessons are taught by singing to the initiates.

For the fourth ceremony, the casting off of uncleanliness, a pool is dammed in a river. The initiates are required to swim four times through an arch built underwater. The boys then scramble after apples that have been scattered on the ground. Those who collect the most apples are expected to be most successful in cattle raids.

The fifth ceremony is the "coming forth."

This is the big festivity at which the initiates come out of seclusion. Each initiate chooses a member of the opposite sex to act as brother or sister to "open the road to adulthood." The brother or sister greets the initiate at the door of the ceremonial hut and leads him or her out to the grounds where there is a procession. The person whom the initiate chooses is considered really a brother or sister and therefore cannot marry the initiate.

Still another ritual is required before the initiates are allowed to marry. The procession of initiates circles a herd of cattle four times, and a priest blesses the herd. Then the ceremony is repeated around the public altar. The girls twist ropes of grass, then untwist them, as they sing. Finally they are told that they are adults, and they pray to have many children. The priest breaks their walking sticks and gives the bottom half to the initiates. These broken sticks must be carried until the final rite, when the initiates' hair is cut for the first time in six months.

The initiation of Kipsigis girls is similar to the boys' ceremonies. However, within three days of her initiation she becomes engaged to be married. A man old enough to marry informs his own parents and the girl's parents of his intention to marry her. In Kipsigis tradition, a young couple intending to marry have some say in the matter.

BEER AS A KIPSIGIS SOCIAL CUSTOM

Almost no Kipsigis ceremony or social gathering is complete without beer. It is also used as payment for work or as trade for goods or services. If a man's wife is pregnant but his cows are not giving milk, he can hold a beer party, and all those who attend must bring milk to the new mother. If there is a disaster and someone needs help building a new hut, he is expected to pay the friends who help him with beer.

There are three kinds of beer parties: ceremonial, village, and private. At each of them, beer is poured into a communal pot, and everyone who is allowed to drink at the gathering sits around the pot on stools or mats. Each drinker has a tube, five to twelve feet long, made of a hollowed-out stalk of the plant *rogaret* and fitted at the bottom with a sieve. An important rule of etiquette governs the *rogaret*: A guest must never step over one. If his neighbor is drinking and the guest wants to pass him, he must wait for the neighbor to lift his tube so that he may go underneath.

At beer parties people discuss village matters, tell stories, sing, and spend time with friends. In fact, everyone is so eager to be invited to a beer gathering that private parties are kept secret until the last minute. If uninvited people show up, they must present themselves to the host. If he decides the new guest is acceptable, he says *Itoch*, meaning "Come up." The behavior of guests is always friendly but quiet and respectful, with only one guest speaking at a time. If the feeling of friendship becomes very strong, one of the elders may reach across the circle and shake the hand of another guest, saying "Let us greet each other." Then all the guests shake each other's hands.

Women are allowed to attend beer parties, but usually choose not to. However, women have a very important role in the gatherings: They make the beer. Kipsigis beer is started with coarse flour mixed with water. This mixture is buried in a pit lined with wild banana leaves. When it has been covered with earth for up to eighteen days, it is roasted. This substance is called *mayuwek*. The *mayuwek* is then mixed with malt to form beer.

The Kipsigis way of drinking beer.

The girls must also go through a ritual called "the frightening." Warriors come during the night, sound bull-roarers, and frighten the initiates as they sleep. It is intended as a trial of endurance and stress. In another rite, the initiate's little finger is tied and the thong pulled tight. This is to remind her that she has been sworn to secrecy. At the coming-out ceremony, a girl initiate's brother takes off her veil in public and anoints her with clarified butter.

chapter

5

MARRIAGE AND FAMILY

THE LIFE OF A KIPSIGIS BOY OR GIRL BEFORE marriage involves training for the responsibilities of adulthood. Sharp differences exist between boys and girls in the types of training they receive.

Boys are trained in the laws of the community and attend public meetings from which women are excluded. Much of their time is spent herding cattle, sheep, and goats, lending a hand during harvests, and training for the *Puriet*, or army. They also engage in competitions to win the favor of beautiful girls.

Girls, however, are constantly warned to keep their virginity until marriage. They are forbidden to conceive children before initiation, although after initiation that is acceptable. In the past, a child born to an uninitiated girl was choked before it drew its first breath, before the spirit of

Boys are trained for the *Puriet*, or army.

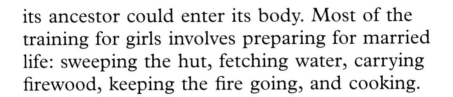

its ancestor could enter its body. Most of the training for girls involves preparing for married life: sweeping the hut, fetching water, carrying firewood, keeping the fire going, and cooking.

▼ MARRIAGE AND CHILDBIRTH ▼

A Kipsigis man can have as many wives as he can afford to take care of. This is called polygamy. A man's first wife is his chief wife, and he seeks her approval before taking a second. Each wife has her own house.

It is important that a family's wealth be kept within that family. If only daughters have been born, either the youngest or the favorite daughter remains at home unmarried. In that way the wealth is not passed on to another family by her marriage.

To marry a Kipsigis woman, a man must give gifts, or bridewealth, to the woman's parents. A typical bridewealth is three cattle and three sheep or goats. The bridewealth is not necessary to the completion of marriage. It is principally a means to cement the relationship between two families. If a woman fails to bear children, the bridewealth must be returned to the husband. This puts pressure on the woman, who must stay in her marriage, no matter the personal cost, so that her parents may keep the bridewealth.

When a childless couple become too old for

Married Kipsigis women are distinguished, in part, by long earrings of intertwined pearls sewn onto leather.

When a couple become too old to bear children, the man can marry a younger wife.

childbearing, the man is allowed to marry a younger wife. If this fails, the older wife can find another man for the younger wife in order to conceive children. In Kipsigis custom, the "marriage" is between the two women. The children's biological father is approved by the childless wife, her own family, and her husband's family. Childbirth is very important to the Kipsigis because they believe that the spirit of a dead ancestor is carried on in the child.

Traditionally, a marriage could not be ended among the Kipsigis. A woman was married into the husband's family, not only to the husband. If a husband died, a kind of "inheriting" was practiced. The junior brother nearest the husband in age became responsible for the care of the widow. This involved adoption of her children, inheritance of her property, maintenance and rebuilding of her house, cultivation of her land, and care of her cattle. But the brother-in-law acquired these rights only with the widow's consent. Today, this practice is resorted to only in secret. In most cases, the eldest son inherits the dead man's wealth and provides for his mother's welfare.

▼ DIVORCE ▼

Only a childless couple can go through the ritual of absolute divorce. But a couple cannot get a divorce just because they have not had children. Something must be seriously wrong with the marriage: adultery, refusal to have sex, continuous fighting, conviction of the wife for sorcery, or incompatibility of wife and husband. Two exceptional circumstances can lead to divorce: when people marry from clans that are not allowed to intermarry; and when murder occurs between members of the husband's and wife's respective clans.

▼ THE FAMILY ▼

The typical Kipsigis household consists of husband, wife, and children. The family is made up not only of parents, siblings, and their children, but all members of the kindred group.

The Kipsigis have no terms for aunt or uncle. A person's mother and aunt are both referred to as "mother" and his father and uncle as "father," and all are respected and treated as such. The same is true of grandfathers or granduncles, grandmothers or grandaunts, and so on. Among relatives, the paternal uncle (the father's brother) plays an important role. Boys in particular have to seek his consent before going through rituals such as initiation. The maternal uncle (the mother's brother) is also important. In return for kindness and concern, a young warrior gives his maternal uncle a cow secured by raiding.

Exogamy is another practice among the

Elders are revered and treated with respect.

The once popular custom of wearing this hairstyle and enlarging holes in the ears has become rare among young, unmarried women.

Kipsigis. It is marriage outside a specified group. The three groups within which Kipsigis cannot marry are the clan, the kindred group, and the age-set. A man cannot marry a woman of his own clan unless the clan has more than one totem animal. He cannot marry a woman from certain other clans. And a man and a woman from the same kindred group cannot marry because they are considered to be relatives. A man cannot marry the daughter of a man in his own age-set. He cannot marry a woman in the age-set of his own children; that would be like marrying his own daughter.

It is not considered an offense if a woman continues to keep her old "sweetheart" after her marriage to another man. Also, a man can leave his house and allow a member of his own age-set to mate with his wife. Except for these cases, a married woman is forbidden to have extra-marital sex. If a man finds his wife breaking these rules, he can divorce her if they have no children, or beat her and her lover, if possible. If a man beats his wife often, however, he may be reported to the wife's father or brothers and the wife may leave him.

Rape is considered an outrage against women. A man guilty of such an offense is beaten severely by members of his own age-set and denied important social privileges.▲

chapter

6

EUROPEAN CONTACT AND COLONIAL RULE

IN THE MIDDLE OF THE 19TH CENTURY THE Kipsigis came into contact with Arab and Swahili traders on the caravan routes that ran from the coast of East Africa to Uganda in the interior. From then on trade in metal ornaments, beads, and foreign cloth developed with these coastal traders.

By 1889 a British trading company, the Imperial East Africa Company, had set up offices in East Africa. Soon afterward, British officers arrived to survey land for the construction of a railway from the coastal city of Mombasa to the great wealth of Uganda. The Kipsigis resisted the invasion of British settlers. They joined with the neighboring Nandi people in attempts to sabotage the project. British troops were sent periodically to put down Kipsigis and Nandi protests, often violently. When the railway was

Contact with Arab and Swahili traders brought metal ornaments, beads, and foreign cloth to the Kipsigis.

completed in 1901, the British seized a strip of land one mile wide on each side of the railway and declared it Crown Lands. This was the beginning of the confiscation of Kipsigis land by British settlers; it was to go on for the next seventy years.

Within seventeen years after the first contact with the Kipsigis in 1889, the British had established their domination. The Kipsigis way of life was changed from a mostly pastoral economy to one of agriculture.

Before the colonial period, the Kipsigis had grown millet and vegetables to supplement the food they got from their cattle. The British introduced corn in 1906.

Because of the increase in farming, there came to be more private ownership of land. This was a new concept to the Kipsigis. The traditional peacemakers of the *kokwet* did not have power to make laws for it. In addition, the British restricted the traditional movement of Kipsigis men and their herds in search of water and grazing areas. Therefore, the British courts had to handle a large number of land cases.

Other aspects of life were also affected by the British. The division of labor between men and women was altered. Traditionally, women had cultivated the land and performed all household duties while men herded cattle and made war. Now both men and women were milking cows,

PLANTS AND ANIMALS IN KIPSIGIS BELIEFS

Plants

The grass called *seretiot* grows in the forest areas of Kipsigisland. The Kipsigis used it to decide when it was lucky or unlucky to hold ceremonies. *Seretiot* takes eight to ten years to grow and flower, and the flowering takes three years. It may be that Kipsigis age-sets follow the blossoming cycle of *seretiot*. The plant flowers once, then dies. Initiation ceremonies never took place in the year after flowering, because that period was associated with illness and death.

The *sasuriet* (wild banana) is important because its leaves are used to make beer. But it is also sacred because of a Kipsigis proverb: "Do not take shelter under a leafy canopy and then cut it down when it stops raining." The saying reminds the Kipsigis never to take kindnesses for granted.

Animals

Some animals are dangerous and are shown great respect. The Kipsigis may have two names for such an animal, one for everyday use and a special one for use when the animal can hear. A Kipsigis legend tells of an animal called *chemosit*, either a hyena or a cheetah. When men were near this animal they would call it *kononet*. *Ongenyot* (elephants) are called by the respectful name *kiptechit* when they are nearby, because of their great size.

If an animal begins to behave strangely, it is called *sogornotet*. For example, the name *sogornotet* is given when an animal bites its young, wraps its tail around a tree, or sticks out and slithers its tongue like a snake. Such are killed and their meat is not eaten.

herding cattle, and planting, weeding, and reaping crops. Livestock raiding was forbidden. Many children went to work on European farms at the age of eight or nine, often without the permission of their father. Some young men even married without their father's aid. These developments undermined the family structure.

The British administration also interfered in Kipsigis cultural life. For example, girls were required to go to initiation much younger. But they still followed the Kipsigis custom of being married soon after initiation. Therefore they often became wives of men many decades older. This led to a weakening of Kipsigis marriage.

Until the 1930s, the Kipsigis were not greatly affected by developments in the rest of the world. By the 1940s, however, they could not always make a living in traditional ways. They often had to take work in farmers' fields as they migrated to areas where cash crops were grown. This change was caused by land shortage and by taxation. As a consequence, the Kipsigis became integrated into the total Kenyan economy.

Unhappy with their situation, the Kipsigis formed the Kipsigis Central Association in 1947 to fight for their social, economic, cultural, and political rights. The colonial government feared that such an organization could become another Mau Mau movement.

Kipsigis were forced to turn to farming to survive.

THE ROAD TO KENYAN INDEPENDENCE

When the British colonized Kenya, land that had always been used by Africans was seized by wealthy European settlers. Like the Kipsigis, most of the peoples of Kenya believed that land belonged to all. Many of the Africans were removed to reservations. Others became squatters; they lived on land owned by Europeans and used the land for cattle-grazing and farming in exchange for working for the settlers.

In the 1940s, there was much dissatisfaction among the native peoples of Kenya. The British colonial government began an "agricultural betterment campaign" to gain a bigger profit from farming in Kenya. They forced peasants to work on communal farming projects, which made the Africans lose trust in the government. In addition, the government began to turn out squatters from the land they worked, leaving them with nothing. These two factors were important reasons for the beginning of the movement that came to be known as **Mau Mau**.

Mau Mau was a movement that demanded freedom from British rule and the return of land to the native peoples. The Kikuyu people were responsible for Mau Mau, but the movement made the colonial government take notice of the discontent of all the Kenyan peoples. By 1952 the Mau Mau movement had become very violent. Settlers and officials were injured or killed, and their property was destroyed. Followers of Mau Mau forced their fellow Kikuyu to take an oath against the government. Those who refused found themselves in danger. That year the government arrested many people whom they believed to be Mau Mau leaders.

One of the people arrested was Jomo Kenyatta, the leader of the Kenya African Union (KAU). He had long spoken out in favor of the rights of the African peoples. However, he believed in a moderate and humane approach to revolution, not the violence of Mau Mau. Nevertheless, Kenyatta was imprisoned for fifteen years.

During those years, the pursuit of freedom continued. In 1954 Africans were allowed for the first time to hold positions in the Kenyan government. A year after Kenyatta was released, he was elected Prime Minister of Kenya, but the British would not allow him to take office. Finally in 1963 he did become Prime Minister. On December 12, 1963, Kenya achieved independence, and Kenyatta became its first President.

▼ INDEPENDENCE ▼

Kenya won its independence from Great Britain on December 12, 1963. Most of the land taken by the British was returned to the Kipsigis. From that point on, the people tried to adjust to the new conditions that colonialism had brought to their society. Many of the changes could not be wiped out overnight, but independence brought with it a revival of old Kipsigis customs.

Because central leadership was gone, Kipsigis needed to find a method of settling disputes. The vast majority of disputes had been settled by the neighborhood elders in *kokwet*.

A new form of cooperation has arisen in the *kokwet*. It is called *kibagenge*. The *kibagenge* allows farmers to work with other farmers and lets cattle herders and merchants work together. Capital is needed in a market economy, and *kipagenge* enables Kipsigis to have a stronger economy. This cooperation fits into the Kenyan government's ideology of *harambee* (a Swahili word meaning "let us work together").▲

chapter

7

A VIEW OF THE FUTURE

TODAY MEN WORK IN TOWNS AND VISIT THEIR families only on weekends or once every few months. As a result, the children do not see their fathers very often. The male children are the most affected by this. They miss out on the necessary contact with their fathers, who in traditional life served as their instructors.

▼ POLYGAMY ▼

Christian missionaries and colonial administrators introduced the practice of monogyny (having only one wife) to the Kipsigis. Because some missionaries did not regard a non-Christian marriage as "a marriage in the eyes of God," they encouraged the breakup of strained Kipsigis marriages. In that way the people could be persuaded to marry a Christian in a Christian church. The missionaries failed to

Young Kipsigis males are the most affected by their fathers' absence.

understand two important aspects of traditional Kipsigis culture. First, they did not understand the Kipsigis concept of the "extended family" and how the household was organized around that family. Second, they failed to realize how complicated it was to end a Kipsigis marriage. Today, the older missions are still faced with the dilemma. The newer missions, such as the Finnish Pentecostal Church, marry polygamists who show signs of Christian faith. It is becoming more common for Christian Kipsigis to take second and third wives. Obviously, polygamy will continue to exist in Kipsigi culture.

▼ POPULATION GROWTH ▼

Vaccination and other Western medical and hygienic practices are now in use in Kipsigis society. Women are also having more babies, so it is likely that the birthrate will continue to grow. Traditionally, the Kipsigis have preferred not to have more children than they can take care of. A growing population will cause a conflict with this ideal.

▼ BRIDEWEALTH ▼

The bridewealth was traditionally a gift of cattle to cement relations between a husband and his wife's parents. Today, the bridewealth is money that pays for the daughter's education. It is easy to see why many parents prefer to have a

Despite all the changes that have taken place, Kipsigis have maintained
many aspects of their tradition.

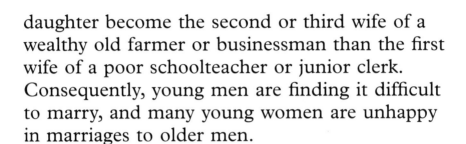

daughter become the second or third wife of a wealthy old farmer or businessman than the first wife of a poor schoolteacher or junior clerk. Consequently, young men are finding it difficult to marry, and many young women are unhappy in marriages to older men.

▼ CONCLUSION ▼

Despite the many changes that have taken place, certain aspects of Kipsigis tradition have survived. The *kokwet* still has authority at the village level. The absence of a centralized form of government fosters a spirit of compromise and shows the Kipsigis' continued belief in equality. These aspects should serve as a stabilizing force in Kipsigis society. The Kipsigis are also learning about their own heritage and are making efforts to return to some of their traditional beliefs and ways of life.▲

Glossary

bridewealth Payment made by a man to the parents of the woman he plans to marry.

circumcision Removal of the prepuce or foreskin of a boy's penis.

exogamy Marriage outside of a specific group as required by custom or law.

hereditary rule Procedure for receiving or passing on something (e.g., wealth).

initiation The rites, ceremony, and ordeal that prepare boys and girls for marriage.

***ipinda* (age-set)** System that defines the duties and privileges of each generation and regulates the social behavior of the Kipsigis.

kibagenge Derived from the word *agenge,* which means "one," it is a cooperative enterprise.

kokwet Kipsigis village.

Mau Mau Liberation movement that advocated violence as a means to pursue political and anticolonial causes in Kenya.

***orkoiyot* (plural *orkoik*)** Ritual leader of the Kipsigis.

poriosiek Kipsigis military unit.

Puriet The Kipsigis army.

totemism Worship of sacred objects, e.g., animals and plants.

For Further Reading

Dramon, Stanley, and Burke, Fred G., eds. *The Transformation of East Africa*. New York: Basic Books, 1966.

Greenberg, Joseph H. *The Languages of Africa* (International Journal of American Linguistics, Part II, vol. 29. no. 1, January). Bloomington: Indiana University Press, 1963.

Gulliver, P. H. *Tradition and Transition in East Africa*. Berkeley: University of California Press, 1969.

Harlow, Vincent, and Cliver, E. M., eds. *History of East Africa* (vol. II). London: Oxford University Press, 1965.

Murdock, George Peter. *Africa: Its People and Their Culture History*. New York: McGraw-Hill, 1959.

Mwanzi, Henry A. *A History of the Kipsigis*. Nairobi: East African Literature Bureau, 1977.

Nelson, Harold D., ed. *Kenya: A Country Study*. Washington, DC: Foreign Area Studies Division, The American University, 1984.

Ogot, Bethwell A. *Historical Dictionary of Kenya*. Metuchen, NJ, and London: The Scarecrow Press, Inc., 1981.

Ojany, Francis F., and Reuben B. Ogendo. *Kenya: A Study in Physical and Human Geography*. Nairobi: Longman Kenya Ltd., 1973.

Oliver, Roland, and Gervase Mathew, eds. *History of East Africa* (vol. I). London: Oxford University Press, 1963.

Orchardson, Ian. *The Kipsigis*. A. T. Matson, ed. Nairobi: East African Literature Bureau, 1961.

Peristiany, J. G. *The Social Institutions of the Kipsigis*. New York: The Humanities Press, 1939/1964.

Index

A
adultery, 42
age-grades, 20
age-set (*ipinda*), 19–20, 22, 35, 44–45
agriculture, 17–18, 36
animals, dual names for, 49
Asis (deity), 23

B
beer, as social custom, 32
boyhood, 20
Boyot ab Tumda (high priest), 25
bridewealth, 38, 56
British colonial rule, 17–18, 23, 46–53

C
cattle-herding, 14, 17, 36, 48
cattle, origin of, 16
chebsogeyot (female doctor), 26
Chemoiben, battle of, 10
Chepalungu, 14
childbirth, 38–41
circumcision, 25, 28–29
clan
  descent through, 20–22
  marriage within, 44
cleansing, rite of, 30
climate, 14
crops, 14, 48
curses, 13
customs, tribal, 29, 30

D
divorce, 41–42

E
elderhood, 20
emotinwek (districts), 17
endurance, physical, 28–29, 33
exogamy, 42–45

F
family, 42–45
  extended, 56
food, from herds, 17

G
girls
  "frightening" ritual for, 33
  initiation of, 31
Gusii, 10, 18, 22–23

I

independence, Kenyan, 18,
52–53
initiation, 19–20, 28–35,
50

K

Kalenjin, 11–12
Kapkoros (public worship),
35
Kenyatta, Jomo, 52
Kericho District, 14
kibagenge, 53
kindred group, 44
Kipsigis Central Association,
50
Kipsigis–Nandi Language
Committee, 12
kisgisik (basket), 9
kokwet, 19, 23, 48, 53, 58

L

laibon (diviner), 26
land, seizure of, 18, 48
language, 11–12

M

magic, 26
marriage, 28, 36–45, 50,
56
Mau Mau, 50, 52
music, 27

N

name, origin of, 9
Nandi, 11, 46

O

"ox-name," boy's, 14–15

P

Peelkut district, 17
plants, 49
polygamy, 38, 54–56
ponindet (magician), 26
population, 11, 56
poriosiek (army unit),
22
proverbs, 13
Pureti district, 17
Puriet (army), 22–23,
36

R

rape, 45
religion, 23–26
riddles, 13
rituals
initiation, 28–31
secret, 28, 33

S

sexual relations, 28
extramarital, 45
refusal of, 42
society, organization of,
19–26
sorcery, 42
Sot, 10, 17
spirit
good or bad, 26
immortal, 25, 41
sun worship, 26

T

totem animal, 22
totemism, 26
townships, development of,
    17–18
traditions, 17–18
  oral, 13
  return to, 58

V

virginity, 36

W

Waldai district, 17
war, 22–23, 48
  rules of, 19
  warriorhood, 20

ABOUT THE AUTHOR
Abdul Karim Bangura was born in Bo, Sierra Leone. He has studied at several universities worldwide, and holds doctorate degrees in Political Science, Social Science, Policy Science, and Linguistics.

Dr. Bangura is currently the Director of The African Institution, the Chairperson of the Research Methodology Scetion of the African Studies Association, a member of the Review Committee of the African Books Publishing Record, and a member of the Editorial Board of the Sierra Leone Review. He is the author of numerous titles, including *Research Methodology and Afrian Studies* and *United States— African Relations—1980 to the Present*. Dr. Bangura speaks, read, and writes Italian, Spanish, French, German, Swedish, and many African languages.

PHOTO CREDITS
AP/Wide World Photo (p. 51); CFM. Nairobi (all other photos)

PHOTO RESEARCH
Vera Ahmadzadeh with Jennifer Croft

DESIGN
Kim Sonsky